THE
SPIRITUAL WAY
BOOK ONE

BY
MOTHER BOLTON
RELIGIOUS OF THE CENACLE
ASSOCIATE PROFESSOR, DEPARTMENT OF EDUCATION
FOR THE TEACHING OF CHRISTIAN DOCTRINE
FORDHAM UNIVERSITY
NEW YORK CITY

2020
ST. AUGUSTINE ACADEMY PRESS
HOMER GLEN, ILLINOIS

This book was originally published in 1930
by World Book Company.

This facsimile edition reprinted in 2020
by St. Augustine Academy Press.

Nihil Obstat

REV. ARTHUR J. SCANLAN, S.T.D.
Censor Librorum

Imprimatur

✠ PATRICK CARDINAL HAYES
Archbishop of New York

NEW YORK
December 8, 1929

ISBN: 978-1-64051-106-4

To **His Holiness Pope Pius XI**
On the occasion of
the Fiftieth Jubilee
of his Ordination, this
book is most humbly
DEDICATED

SEGRETERIA DI STATO

DI SUA SANTITA

To the honored Mother Superior General
of the Religious of the Cenacle

The Holy Father accepts with great pleasure the set of four volumes of The Spiritual Way *written by one of your religious to facilitate the teaching of the Catechism in America. His Holiness thanks you with all his heart for this token of whole-hearted veneration and devotion to his august person and expresses his congratulations and fatherly interest in the work.*

Happy to see the good results of this method of teaching the Catechism in the schools of the United States and rejoicing in the belief that these results will be multiplied elsewhere, His Holiness with all his heart gives, as a mark of his paternal affection and as a guarantee of the best of heavenly blessings upon this work, his special Apostolic Benediction.

E. Card. Pacelli

Secretary of State to His Holiness Pius XI

TRANSLATED FROM THE ORIGINAL IN FRENCH

The Spiritual Way Series goes forth to all boys and girls with a greeting to each one and a prayer that God, the Author of Light and Love and Power, will be their Guide as they advance from one book of the series to the other.

For when God is Guide, a boy or girl always grows in His Light and Love and Power. And this Light and Love and Power are never kept within himself. He becomes a Light-bearer, and brings the Light of God wherever he goes.

So may millions of boys and girls carry such an abundance of God's Light and Love and Power that they will make this whole world bright and beautiful with light and love.

The Author

Contents

Contents

PROJECTS AND TESTS

·.·THE·LORD·HE·IS·GOD·.·.·HE·MADE·US·.·

GOD THE CREATOR

TOPIC ONE

LET us make believe that you are a carpenter.

Suppose you are going to make a box.

What things do you need to make a box?

Boards, nails, a hammer, and other things.

Or perhaps you want to make a wagon.
What must you have to make the wagon?

Boards, nails, wheels, and other things.

Now suppose someone asks you to make either a box or a wagon.

But you have no boards or nails.
What would you answer?

*I cannot make either the box or the wagon unless
I have the things I need to make it.*

Let us make believe that you want to make a dress
for a doll.
What must you have to make the dress?

Cloth, thread, a needle, and shears.

Suppose you are going to make a doll's hat.

What must you have to make the hat?

A frame, ribbons, a needle, and thread.

Suppose someone asks you to make a doll's dress.
But you have no cloth, no needle, no thread.
What would you answer?

*I cannot make the doll's dress unless I have the
things I need to make it.*

Whenever you want to make anything, what do you
need before you can make it?

I need the things that I must use to make it.

MAKING THINGS OUT OF NOTHING

Suppose you had nothing at all, what could you
make?

I could not make anything.

So you see, *you* cannot make something out of
nothing.

Do you know any boy or girl who can make things out of nothing?

No.

Do you know any man or woman who can make things out of nothing?

No.

But there is Someone Who has the power to make things out of nothing.

For, in the beginning, when God wanted the first trees and flowers and grass to grow upon the earth, He said:
" Let the earth bring forth the green herb . . . and the fruit tree . . . And it was so done." (Genesis 1 : 11)

Genesis, which means beginning, tells you that I found those words that God said in the first book of *The Bible*.

And in the very beginning when God wanted the sun, the moon, and the stars, He said:
" Let there be lights made in the . . . heaven . . .
And it was so done.
And God made two great lights: a . . . light to rule the day; and a . . . light to rule the night: and the stars.'' (Genesis 1 : 14–16)
What is the light that rules the day?
What do you call the light that rules the night?

In the very beginning God also said:
" Let the waters bring forth the creeping creature . . . and the fowl that may fly over the earth. . . .
And God created the great whales, and every living and moving creature which the waters brought forth.'' (Genesis 1 : 20, 21)
And when God wanted the very first cattle and creeping things, and the beasts of the earth, He said:
" Let the earth bring forth . . . cattle and creeping

things, and beasts of the earth . . . And it was so done." (Genesis 1 : 24)

So you see that in the very beginning when God wanted the land, and everything growing upon it, such as trees, flowers, and grass, He made them out of nothing.

> " For he spoke, and they were made :
> he commanded and they were created."

This Bible verse is found in Psalm 32.
In The Bible there are one hundred and fifty of the most beautiful poems ever written.
These poems are called Psalms.

And in the very beginning God also made the seas, and all the fish in the seas, out of nothing.

> " For he spoke, and they were made."

And God made the sun, the moon, and the stars, out of nothing.

"For he spoke, and they were made."

We say that God made the world out of nothing. For the earth with everything living upon it — the seas and everything in them — the heavens, where the sun, the moon, and the stars are — all these taken together are called *the world*.

You know that God did not create *you* just as you are now. For as you grow, you change. And it is the same with the world that God created. Changes are always taking place.

Because God made the world out of nothing, He is called the Creator.

YOUR PROJECT BOOK

The Spiritual Way will give you careful directions for making a new book of your own. *The Spiritual Way* calls this book your Project Book.

But you may give another title to your book if you wish to do this.

You will want your Project Book to be a beautiful and useful book. So everything you write in it should have a neat appearance and a proper heading.

Begin your Project Book by writing in it some of the things that happened when God spoke.

Copy the following statement in your Project Book, filling in the blank spaces.

God is the —— of heaven and —— and of —— things.

Look in your Catechism for the question: "Who is God?"

See if the statement you have written in your Project Book is the same as the Catechism answer to this question.

CREATURES OF GOD

Everything that the Creator makes is called a *creature*. This means that the sun, the moon, and the stars are creatures of God.

The earth and everything on it are also creatures of God.

And the seas and everything in them are creatures of God.

Write in your Project Book what is meant by *Creator* and *creature*.

Now you have been thinking about many of God's creatures.

See if you can answer the questions below. They are questions about creatures.

What did God create to give us light by day? By night?

What did He create to grow upon the earth to make it very beautiful?

Besides people, which creatures of God walk and run upon the earth?

Which ones fly in the air?

Which ones live in the sea?

Some of God's creatures can solve problems in arithmetic and in other subjects. Which creatures can do this?

Some of the creatures you have named are more important than others. Which are the most important?

Write the answers to all of these questions in your Project Book.

ANGELS AND MEN

Among all the creatures everywhere upon the earth,
which do you think are the most important?

I think that people are the most important.

Besides people, or human beings, God has made
other beings. They are very important, too.
These other beings do not have bodies, as we have.
So they could be all around us, and we would not be
able to see them.
Perhaps you have already heard about these other
important beings. What are they called?

They are called angels.

The most important creatures of God are called
chief creatures. Which, then, are the chief creatures
of God living upon the earth?

*People are the chief creatures of God living upon
the earth.*

What other creatures of God are also called chief creatures?

Angels are also called chief creatures of God.

Look at the angels in the picture. You see that in pictures angels look like beautiful people with wings.

But everyone knows that angels are not really like the pictures, because angels have no bodies.
So we never can see angels unless God wants us to see them.

The word " angel " means messenger.
And God has sent angels to earth with very important messages.

Two of the angels who came to earth with important messages from God are called Gabriel and Raphael.
And Michael is a prince among the angels.

Copy the following statements in your Project Book, filling in the blank spaces.

The word "angel" means ——.

—— and —— are two angels sent to earth with messages from God.

The —— creatures of God are men and ——.

Look in your Catechism for this question: "Which are the chief creatures of God?"

See if the statement you have written in your Project Book is the same as the Catechism answer to this question.

In this Catechism answer, the word "men" means all men, women, and children.

RIGHT AND WRONG TEST : CREATOR AND CREATURE

Some of these sentences are true.
Some of them are not true.
What are the numbers of the six sentences that are not true ?

I can make things out of nothing.	1
God can make things out of nothing.	2
Angels are chief creatures of God.	3
Horses are chief creatures of God.	4
An angel is a creature.	5
God is a creature.	6
My mother created a cake.	7
God created the world.	8
We can see people because they have bodies.	9
We can see angels because they have bodies.	10
All creatures can work problems in arithmetic.	11
People can work problems in arithmetic.	12

Read aloud each of the six sentences that are not true. Now read them again, but change the words to make each sentence tell the truth.

Write these twelve true sentences in your Project Book.

WHY GOD MADE ALL THINGS

The boy in the picture made his kite out of things that were given to him.

To whom does the kite belong — to him, or to some other boy?

The kite belongs to the boy who made it.

Suppose a girl made a dress for her doll, and all the things she used belonged to her.

To whom would the doll's dress belong — to the girl who made it, or to some other girl?

It would belong to the girl who made it.

You know that God made heaven and earth and all things, out of nothing.

To Whom, then, do heaven and earth and all things belong?

Heaven and earth and all things belong to God.

You also know that God created the angels.
Then, to Whom do the angels belong?

The angels belong to God.

And you know that God created all men, women, and children.
To Whom, then, do all men, women, and children belong?

All men, women, and children belong to God.

To Whom do you belong?

I belong to God.

In The Bible, in a book called Proverbs, there is a verse which tells us *why God made all things*.
Why do you think God made all things?
The Bible verse says:
" The Lord hath made all things for himself."
(Proverbs 16 : 4)

Write this Bible verse in your Project Book.

A TEST: "HE MADE US, AND NOT WE OURSELVES"

There are ten sentences in this test.
Copy the sentences in your Project Book.
Then write the correct answers in the *Who or What* column.
For example, the answer to question 1 is *God*.

	Who or What
1. Who made the world?	*God*
2. What is God called because He made the world out of nothing?	
3. What name is given to anything that the Creator makes?	
4. What are you called because God made you?	
5. Who is the Creator?	
6. What are the names of God's chief creatures?	
7. To Whom do heaven and earth and all things belong?	
8. To Whom do you belong?	
9. What do you call the chief creatures of God living upon the earth?	
10. What does the word "Genesis" mean?	

Show what you have written in your Project Book to your teacher or someone at home.

How many of your answers are correct?

WE ARE HIS PEOPLE

The following Bible verses and the poem on pages 18
and 19 will help you to remember that God is your
Creator, and that you belong to Him.
Copy the Bible verses and the poem in your Project
Book.

The first Bible verse is from Psalm 99.

> " Know ye that the Lord he is God:
> He made us, and not we ourselves.
> We are his people and the sheep
> of his pasture."

You will find this Bible verse set to music on
page 23 of this book. Sing it to someone at home.

The other Bible verse is from Psalm 148.

> " Praise ye the Lord, all his angels:
> Praise ye him, O sun and moon:
> Praise ye him, all ye stars and light.
> Kings of the earth, and all people:
> Young men, and maidens:
> Let the old with the younger praise
> the name of the Lord."

ALL things
    bright and
        beautiful,
All creatures great and
        small,
All things wise and
        wonderful,
The Lord God made
    them all.

Each little flower
    that opens,
Each little bird that
        sings,
He made their glowing
        colors,
He made their tiny
        wings.

The cold wind in the
winter,
The pleasant summer
sun,
The ripe fruits in the
garden,
He made them every
one.

He gave us eyes to
see them,
And lips that we might
tell
How great is God
Almighty,
Who has made all
things well.

Cecil Francis Alexander.

A BIBLE PUZZLE: CREATION

The parts of sentences in column A are to be completed from the parts in column B.

Work the puzzle this way.

Read the unfinished sentence marked 1.

Then look down column B. You see that the first five statements do not belong with the unfinished sentence numbered 1, because they would not make a true sentence. But the next one, Genesis, is right.

Copy the sentence in your Project Book.

Work out the second sentence the same way. Write the completed sentence in your Project Book.

Then do the rest of this Bible puzzle.

COLUMN A *Sentences to finish*	COLUMN B *From The Bible*
1. The book of The Bible which tells about how God created the world is —	11. "Let the earth bring forth the fruit tree."
2. When God made the sun, the moon, and the stars, He said —	12. "Let there be lights made in the . . . heaven."
3. The verse from The Bible which tells how God created all things in the world is —	13. "We are his people and the sheep of his pasture."
4. When God wanted fruit trees upon the earth, He said —	14. "Let the earth bring forth cattle and creeping things and beasts of the earth."

5. When God wanted to make anything in the world, He spoke —

15. "Know ye that the Lord he is God: he made us."

6. When God made cattle and creeping things of the earth, He said —

16. Genesis.

7. The Bible verse which tells that God made us is —

17. "And it was so done."

8. The Bible verse which tells that we are God's people and His sheep is —

18. "For he spoke and they were made."

9. God told us that He made all things for Someone, when He said —

19. Psalms.

10. You will find many beautiful poems in the book of The Bible called —

20. "The Lord hath made all things for himself."

Well! That test was hard, wasn't it?

STANDARDS

If you had 6 answers right, you PASSED.
If you had 7 answers right, that was GOOD.
If you had 8 answers right, that was VERY GOOD.
If you had 9 answers right, that was EXCELLENT.
If you had 10 answers right, that was PERFECT.

SOME BIBLE VERSES SET TO MUSIC
Gregorian Chant

The music in this lesson, called Gregorian Chant, is like the music which a very holy Pope, Saint Gregory, arranged for Catholic children who lived over thirteen hundred years ago.

There are eight different tones which Pope Gregory taught as the best music for Bible verses.

Pope Pius XI asked boys and girls in all countries to learn to sing these tones. Saint Gregory's *first tone* is the music to which the Bible verse, " Know ye that the Lord he is God," has been set for you to sing.

Melodies

The second part of this music lesson is a melody. And you will find it easy to sing, because it is written like the rote songs that you have been singing in school.

THE LORD HE IS GOD

King David, who wrote these Bible verses which have been set to music for you, was a shepherd.

And God called David from his sheep to be the king and shepherd of His people Israel.

So when David wrote these verses to give praise to God, he thought of all people as sheep and God as the Good Shepherd.

Gregorian Chant: First Tone

PSALM 99 : 3

Know ye that the Lord he is God : he made us, and not we our - selves.

Melody: CORNELIA S. CRANE

We are his peo-ple and the sheep of his pas - ture.

All the melodies in *The Spiritual Way* were composed by Cornelia S. Crane for her grandchildren.

GOD OUR LOVING FATHER

TOPIC TWO

IN Topic One you learned two words that sound much alike. See if you remember them. You know that God made heaven and earth, and all things, out of nothing.

What is God called because He made heaven and earth, and all things, out of nothing?

God is called the Creator.

Do you know the other word that sounds something like Creator?
It is the name for anything that the Creator has made. What is the word?

Creature.

Name some of God's creatures.

Animals, flowers, the sun, and the stars.

When we were talking about God's creatures, you learned that some of them are more important than others.

Which are the most important or the chief creatures of God ?

Angels and people.

So you see that God created *you* to be one of His *chief* creatures.

And your Creator has given you some wonderful gifts.

Because you have one of these gifts, there are many things that you can do.

For example, you can see.   You can write.   You can breathe.

With what do you see ?

My eyes.

With what do you write ?

My hands.

With what do you breathe ?

My lungs.

Your eyes, hands, and lungs are all parts of this one gift.

What is the name of the gift ?

My body.

Besides your body, the Creator has given you many other wonderful gifts.

Three of these gifts the Creator did not give to horses, dogs, or other animals.

And these three gifts are not like eyes or hands or any other part of the body.

In this lesson let us learn about the three gifts that are not like eyes or hands or any other part of the body.

THE POWER TO KNOW AND THE POWER TO CHOOSE

Let us suppose that you want to write a letter to someone.

Of course, you must have a pencil, or a pen and ink, and paper.

But before you know just what you are going to say in the letter, what must you do?

I must think.

After you think for a while about what you are going to say in the letter, will you then know what to write?

I will then know what to write.

In school your teacher often gives you hard problems in arithmetic.

What must you do to find the correct answer?

I must think.

After you *think* for a while, if the problem is not too hard for you, will you then *know* how to find the correct answer?

I will then know how to find the correct answer.

Now let us suppose that you have some money to spend today.
You were given the money to buy a toy.
What toy would you buy?
Why would you buy that toy?

Suppose your teacher had a box of pictures. And she told you to take one of these pictures.
Which picture would you take?

Whenever you pick out a toy or a picture or something you like, *you are choosing*.

You know what to say in a letter, and you can solve a problem in arithmetic, because your Creator has given you the *power to think and to know*.

The power to think and to know is one of the gifts which the Creator gives to *people*.

But He does not give this same kind of power to other creatures living upon the earth.

You can pick out the toy and the picture you like best because your Creator has given you the *power to choose*.

The power to choose is another of the gifts which the Creator gives to people.

But He does not give this same kind of power to other creatures living upon the earth.

Now, if someone asks you to tell what power your Creator has given you so that you can write a letter or solve a problem in arithmetic, what will you answer?

I will answer: God has given me the power to think and to know.

Or if someone asks you to tell what power God has given you so that you can pick out the toy or the picture you like best, what will you answer?

I will answer: God has given me the power to choose.

When God created you, He gave you these two gifts:

The power to think and to know, and
The power to choose.

A Test: How I Use the Power to Know and the Power to Choose

The statements in column A on page 30 can be completed with statements in column B.

For example, No. 1 can be completed with No. 13 in column B. The complete sentence will read: I can write and see and talk *because* my Creator has given me a body.

Complete the other sentences in the same way. Write the completed sentences in your Project Book.

Show what you have written in your Project Book to someone at home.

How many of your answers are correct?

STANDARDS
7 correct answers: Perfect
6 correct answers: Good
5 correct answers: Fair
4 correct answers: Poor
Mark your score.

COLUMN A		COLUMN B
1. I can write and see and talk	*because*	8. my Creator has given me the power to choose.
2. I can solve problems in arithmetic	*because*	9. the Creator did not give the power to think, to know, and to choose to creatures that have no life.
3. I can pick out the things I like best	*because*	10. they are the chief creatures of God.
4. Horses, dogs, or other animals cannot work problems	*because*	11. my Creator has given me the power to think and to know.
5. A stone or a tree cannot think or know or choose	*because*	12. I told her that I have the power to think and to know.
6. People and angels can think and know and choose	*because*	13. my Creator has given me a body.
7. Susan knows why I can write a letter or solve a problem in arithmetic	*because*	14. the Creator did not give to any animal the power to think and to know.

GOD'S LIGHT

Now let us think about the third gift which your Creator has given to you.

At the beginning of your life you did not have this third gift.

But your Creator gave you this gift when you were *baptized*.

The Bible tells us in the book of Saint John that

"God is Light."

But when The Bible tells us that *God is Light*, it does not mean light like the sunlight, but a very different kind of light.

The Light of Knowing

Sometimes when grown-up people find out how to solve a problem which they found hard at first, they say, " Now I have light, because I understand it."

And when you *know something*, you also can say that you have light about it.

This kind of light is called your *light of knowing*, because it gives you the power to understand things — which means to know them.

Your light of knowing helps you to know numbers and everything else you want to learn at school or at home.

Now you know about two kinds of light.
What kind of light makes the day bright?

Sunlight makes the day bright.

What kind of light helps you to know about everything that God created?

**My light of knowing helps me to know about
everything that God created.**

The Light of God in Us

There is a third kind of light, and this is God's very best gift to you.

For this kind of light is called the *Light of God*, and it gives you *the power to know God Himself*.

THREE KINDS OF LIGHT

Copy these sentences in your Project Book. Put the name of the right kind of light in the blank spaces.

1. —— is the light which makes the world bright.
2. My light of —— gives me the power to learn numbers and other lessons.
3. When I have the Light of ——, I have the power to know God Himself.
4. My light of —— helps me to know about the things I see in the world.
5. The light that makes the difference between day and night is the ——.
6. The most important kind of light is the Light of ——.

GOD'S BEAUTY

Now read the poem " All Things Bright and Beautiful " on pages 18 and 19.

Who made all the beautiful things which the sunlight helps you to see ?

God made all the beautiful things which the sunlight helps me to see.

But the sunlight cannot help you to see some of the most beautiful things in the world.

For it is not sunlight but the light of knowing which helps a child to see the beauty of his mother's goodness.

A mother's goodness and all kinds of beauty in the world come from God.

For God is the Source of all beauty.

When your light of knowing gives you the power to see the beauty of your mother's goodness, you love that goodness.

And when God's Light gives you the power to see God's Beauty, you *love* His Beauty.

THE LIGHTS WHICH SHOW US BEAUTY

Now copy these sentences about beauty and love in your Project Book. Put the right words in the blank spaces.

1. The sunlight helps me to see all the —— things that God has made. And when I see the —— things that God has made, I will choose them.
2. My light of knowing gives me the power to see the —— of my mother's goodness. And when I see the —— of my mother's goodness, I —— it.
3. God's Light gives me the power to see —— Beauty. And when I see —— Beauty, I —— Him.

THE LIGHT OF GRACE

God, the Father of Lights, lets you share in His Own Light and Beauty.

The Bible tells us in the book of Saint James that "Every best gift . . . is from . . . the Father of lights."

(Saint James 1 : 17)

And you have learned that God's Light in you gives you the power to know and love God Himself.
Saint Thomas calls this gift the *Light of Grace.*
Your Catechism calls it *sanctifying* grace.
When you receive the Light of Grace at Baptism, you receive God's very best gift.

For when the Light of Grace is in you, you are sharing in God's Own Light and Beauty.

God "hath called you out of darkness into his . . . light." (1 Saint Peter 2 : 9)

Why God Loves You Tenderly

When the Light of Grace is in you, God loves you tenderly. He cares for and protects you, as your mother did when she took you in her arms.
For God's Light and Beauty in you make you God's child.
Then God is your most Loving Father.

And when God is your Loving Father, you belong
with Him in His home in heaven, just as any child
on earth belongs in his earthly father's home.

MATCHING TEST : GOD, THE FATHER OF LIGHTS

Finish the sentences in this matching test about God,
the Father of Lights.   Do this in the same way that you
did the Bible puzzle on page 20.
Write the completed sentences in your Project Book.

Sentences to finish	*About God*
1. God is —	down from the Father of Lights.
2. The Light of God gives us the power —	of all beauty.
3. Every best gift is from above, coming —	Lights, he means that every best gift comes from God.
4. God hath called you out of darkness —	Light.
5. God, the Father of Lights, is the Source —	does not mean light like the sunlight.
6. God's Light in me gives —	into . . . light.
7. When Saint James tells us that every best gift comes from the Father of —	to know God Himself.
8. When The Bible tells us that God is Light, it —	me the power to see God's Beauty and to love Him.

MATCHING TEST: THE LIGHT OF GRACE

Sentences to finish | *About the Light of Grace*

1. God's Own Light and Beauty in me —	me share in His Own Light and Beauty.
2. The Light of Grace gives me —	the Light of Grace.
3. The more I have of this Light of God —	God's Beauty, and to love Him.
4. God's best gift to me is —	I was baptized.
5. God's Light of Grace in me gives me the power to see —	the power to love and choose God.
6. When I have the Light of Grace, God lets —	the more power I will have to know God Himself.
7. When God's Own Light and Beauty are in me, God —	with Him in His home in heaven.
8. God gave me the Light of Grace when —	loves me tenderly.
9. When God is my Loving Father, I belong —	make me God's child.

There are 17 numbers in these two tests.

17 correct answers: PERFECT
16 correct answers: EXCELLENT
14 correct answers: GOOD
12 correct answers: FAIR

Mark your score.

THE SOUL AND ITS POWERS.

At the beginning of this Topic you knew that your eyes, hands, and lungs are parts of your body.

Now you have learned about three gifts from God which are not like your eyes or lungs or any other part of your body.

One of these gifts from God gives you the power to think and to know.

And you do not think and know with your body.

You think and know with your soul.

Another gift from God gives you the power to choose.

And you do not choose with your body.

You choose with your soul.

And it is into your *soul*, most of all, that God brings His Own Light and Beauty — His very best gift.

So you see that God has given you a soul as well as a body.

And it is because you have a soul that you have

> *The power to think and to know,*
> *The power to choose, and*
> *The very best gift of sharing in*
> *God's Own Light ana Beauty.*

Here are some questions about the lesson you have been learning.

When you see and talk and play, you use different parts of your body.

But does any part of your body give you the power to think and to know?

No.

Does any part of your body give you the power to choose?

No.

What does give you the power to think and to know, and the power to choose?

My soul gives me the power to think and to know, and the power to choose.

When did God give you these two gifts — the power to think and to know, and the power to choose?

When God created me, He gave me the power to think and to know, and the power to choose.

When did God give you His very best gift — the Light of Grace?

When I was baptized, God gave me the Light of Grace.

When you have God's very best gift, there is a Light and Beauty in your soul which was not there before.

Whose Light and Beauty are then in your soul?

God's Light and Beauty are then in my soul.

When God's Light and Beauty are in your soul,
God is your Father.
You are His loving child.
Now tell what gift made you God's loving child.

*The gift of sharing in God's Light and Beauty
made me His loving child.*

Copy the following statement in your Project Book,
filling in the blank spaces.

—— grace is that grace which makes the soul holy and
pleasing to ——.

Look in your Catechism for the question: "What is sanctifying grace?"

See if the statement you have written in your Project
Book is the same as the Catechism answer to this question.

There is a big Catechism called the Catechism of
the Council of Trent.
That Catechism tells more about God's Light and
Beauty in the soul.
When you are older, you will study that Catechism,
and then you will know all that it says about God's
very best gift to you.

MY SOUL AND THE LIGHT OF GRACE

In the sentences below some words are left out. Put the right words in the blank spaces.

Write the completed sentences in your Project Book.

1. My —— has the power to think and to know.
2. My —— has not the power to think and to know.
3. I choose with my ——.
4. I do not choose with my ——.
5. God gave me the Light of Grace when I was ——.
6. I am God's loving ——.
7. God is my Loving ——.
8. God's Own Light and Beauty are more in my —— than in my body.
9. The gift of sharing in God's Own Light and Beauty makes me God's ——.
10. God gave me the power to think and to know and the power to choose when He —— me.

Show what you have written in your Project Book to your teacher or someone at home.

How many of your answers are correct?

THE KING OF KINGS

Let us learn some verses from The Bible about the King of Kings.

> " Sing praises to our God, sing ye :
> Sing praises to our king, sing ye.
> For God is the king of all the earth."
>
> (Psalm 46 : 7, 8)

You see from these Bible verses that Our Heavenly Father is *King* of all the earth.

For the earth and everything on it belong to Him. And all people who are sharing in God's Own Light and Beauty are His very dear children.

So if you are sharing in God's Own Light and Beauty, *you are the children of the King of all the earth.* You know what the children of an earthly king are called.

What are the boys called ?

The boys are called princes.

What are the girls called ?

The girls are called princesses.

And as you are a child of the King of all the earth, you are really *a prince or a princess of Our Heavenly Father's kingdom.*

And now let us see what every noble prince or princess of God's kingdom must do to be pleasing to his King.

First of all, every noble prince or princess of God's kingdom must love his King.

And if he loves his King, *he will think about Him and talk to Him often during the day*.

And a prince or princess must act in the way that God, his King, wants a prince or princess to act.

Be Brave

Should a prince or princess of Our Heavenly Father's kingdom be brave or cowardly?

A prince or princess of Our Heavenly Father's kingdom should be brave.

Do you think that a noble prince or princess of God's kingdom will always find it easy to be brave?

Here is a story about a boy named William.
William's father left his watch on his desk.
William took the watch to show it to some boys.
One of them broke it.
William quickly put the watch back on his father's desk. He said nothing.
If William had been a brave prince of God's kingdom, what would he have done?
Think of one time when it was hard for you to be brave. What happened that time?

Be Kind

Should a prince or princess of Our Heavenly Father's kingdom be kind and gentle, or unkind and rude?

A prince or princess of Our Heavenly Father's kingdom should be kind and gentle.

Here is a story about a girl named Catherine.
Catherine's mother is very sick.
So Catherine must do the housework and be kind and gentle with the younger children, if the home is to be a happy place while their mother is sick.
What will Catherine do if she is a kind and gentle princess of God's kingdom?

Do you remember any time in your life when it was not easy for you to be kind and gentle?

Be True

Should a prince or princess of Our Heavenly Father's kingdom be truthful or untruthful?

A prince or princess of Our Heavenly Father's kingdom should be truthful.

Here is a story about a boy who proved that he was a prince of God's kingdom.

Thomas's class took a speed test in arithmetic. After the test was finished, the papers were exchanged and corrected by the class.

Thomas's paper was corrected by his friend, Edward. Edward marked the paper 100 per cent.

Thomas looked his paper over. He saw that in an example where he was asked to add dollars and cents, he had added the figures correctly, for his answer was 16825. But the correct answer was $168.25.

Thomas marked his answer wrong, and changed his mark from 100 to 90 per cent.

The captain of Thomas's row asked those who had 100 per cent to stand. Thomas remained seated, although the mark that Edward gave him would have made his row win.

If you had been in Thomas's place, what would you have done?

What would any true prince of God's kingdom do?

A Noble Prince or Princess

What makes you a noble prince or princess of Our Heavenly Father's kingdom?

Write the answer in your Project Book by filling in the blank spaces in the following sentence.

Anyone is a noble prince or princess of Our Heavenly Father's kingdom when he is sharing in God's Own —— and ——.

Now write the other sentences, filling in the blank spaces. You will then have *your motto* as a prince or princess of God's kingdom.

Prince and Princess Motto

1. I love my ——.
2. I will be ——.
3. I will be ——.
4. I will be ——.

OUR TRUE SHIELD AND PROTECTOR

In the days of long ago, every prince of an earthly kingdom who went forth to fight for his king carried a shield.

The prince carried this shield on his left arm so that he could move it in any direction to protect himself when he was fighting for his king.

FOR LOVE OF THE KING :: KIND : TRUE :: BRAVE

Look at the picture of a prince carrying his shield.

Draw this shield in your Project Book.
Then write a paragraph telling why princes of long ago carried shields.

Long, long ago a noble earthly king was sharing in God's Own Light and Beauty, for the Light of Grace was in his soul.
And so he was a true prince of God's kingdom as well as a noble earthly king.
His name was David.

God was well pleased with David.
And God made known to David that He would always protect him in battle and every time he was in any danger.
Ask someone at home to tell you how David fought a great giant, who had made everyone else afraid of him.

David knew that God wanted him to fight this giant and that God would be his Protector.
So David did not carry a shield when he went to fight the giant.
Another way of saying that God was always David's Protector is to say that God was his Shield. (Deuteronomy 33 : 29)

Like David, you are a prince of God's kingdom if the Light of Grace is in your soul.

You do not carry a shield upon your left arm, as the earthly princes of long ago did.

But the same One Who protected David from all dangers protects you.

Who is your Protector and your Shield?

God is my Protector and my Shield.

The Prince's Banner

Sometimes when princes of earthly kingdoms went to battle, they carried banners, on which everyone could see the motto of their king.

Look at the prince in the picture.

Read the words on his banner.

You see this prince has a motto like the one that you have.

Now suppose that this prince

> is a coward,
> is rude and unkind,
> tells a lie.

Then he fails to *uphold the banner and the honor of his king*.

Draw the banner. Be sure to put the prince's motto on it.

MOTTO TEST: BRAVE, KIND, AND TRUE

One word on the banner will solve each of these problems. Copy the problems in your Project Book.

Opposite each problem, in the column marked *Failure*, write the word of your motto which tells the way each boy or girl failed.

	Failure
1. Suppose John ate the cake that his mother had saved for the family supper. John's mother asked him if he knew what had happened to the cake. John said that he did not know.	
2. On Monday mornings Jane was expected to do some housework, so that the woman who worked for her mother could help with the washing. But Jane was rude and disagreeable to the woman.	
3. Suppose James and Michael were running a race. Both boys wanted to win the prize. In running, they passed near each other. James knew that he could trip Michael and no one would see him. He tripped Michael.	
4. Rose and Helen were playing a game at school. Rose hurt Helen so badly that Helen could not go to school the next day. Rose was afraid to tell what she had done. She did not even tell her mother.	
5. Anthony caused trouble in his classroom. His teacher wrote a note to his mother. When Anthony's mother asked him about it, Anthony said that the teacher did not know, but that another boy had caused the trouble.	

"HEARKEN TO THE VOICE OF MY PRAYER"

Who always knows when it is hard for you to be brave, or truthful, or kind and gentle?

God always knows.

When you want Our Loving Father to help you to be brave, or truthful, or kind and gentle, what must you do?

I must ask Him to help me.

Tell the very words that you will say when you ask God to help you to be brave.
How will you ask God to make you kind and gentle?
Tell the words you will say when you ask God to help you to speak the truth.
Here is a prayer that I say when I ask God to help me to be brave and kind and true.

MY PRAYER

> God make me brave.   I can be brave!
> God make me kind.   I should be kind!
> God keep me true.   I must be true!
> Brave, kind, and true — I love my King!

Say this prayer when you find it hard to be brave or kind or true.

Here is a Bible verse for children who have the Light of Grace in their souls. Write it in your Project Book and learn it.

" Walk then as children of the light.
For the fruit of the light is in all
goodness . . . and truth." (Ephesians 5 : 8, 9)

Learn also the Bible verses on page 54.

THE KING OF ALL THE EARTH

In the days of long ago King David and other poets wrote many beautiful poems and songs in praise of God, the great King of all the earth.

One of these songs of praise has been set to music for you so that you may praise God in the beautiful words of the forty-sixth psalm.

Sing joyfully this song of praise to God, the King of Kings.

Gregorian Chant: Second Tone

Sing prais-es to our God, sing ye : sing praises to our king, Sing, sing ye;

Melody: CORNELIA S. CRANE

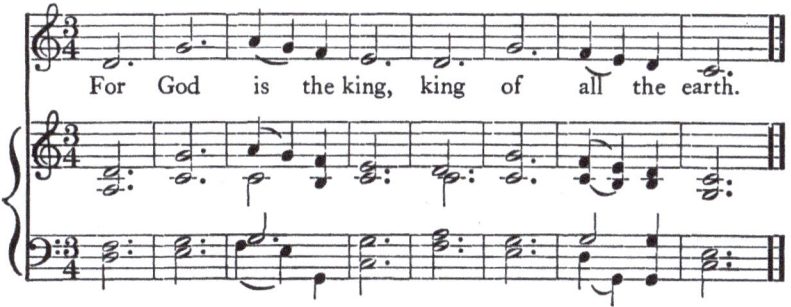

For God is the king, king of all the earth.

"He that saith he is in the light, and hateth his brother, is in darkness even until now."
(1 St. John 2:9)

"My little children, let us not love in word, nor in tongue, but in deed, and in truth."
(1 St. John 3:18)

"I have no greater grace than this, to hear that my children walk in truth."
(3 St. John 1:4)

HOLY ART THOU O GOD HOLY ART THOU O MIGHTY ONE

HOLY · ART · THOU · O · IMMORTAL · ONE · HAVE · MERCY · ON · US

THE ONE WHOSE POWER CAN PROTECT ALL PEOPLE

TOPIC THREE

YOU know that you are one of God's creatures, because He created you.

And because God created you, what do you call Him?

I call God Creator.

You also know that when anyone is sharing in God's Own Light and Beauty he is God's *child*.

And because you are God's child, what do you call God?

I call God Father.

To help you to learn more about God, your Creator
and Loving Father, read this story about something
that God did thousands of years ago.

GOD SHOWS HIS POWER

Thousands of years ago most of the people on the
earth became very, very wicked.
There was none of God's Own Light and Beauty in
their souls.
They were so wicked that God said He was sorry ·
He had made them. And He said that He would
destroy all of them.

But there was a man named Noë who was very
pleasing to God. For God's Light of Grace was in
his soul. And God saved Noë and his family.
God told Noë just how to build a big house boat.
This house boat was called an ark.
And when the ark was built, God told Noë to go
into the ark with his family, and to take two of
every kind of living creature with him.

Then there came a great flood of water, called a
deluge.
It rained and rained so long and so hard that the
water covered the land and destroyed every living

thing except those who were safe in the ark. (Genesis 6, 7, and 8)

Who is the only One mighty enough to have saved Noë and his family in this way?

After the deluge was over, "God spoke to Noë, saying, Go out of the ark. . . .
So Noë went out, he and his sons: his wife, and the wives of his sons with him. And all living things . . . went out of the ark.
And Noë built an altar unto the Lord."
Noë built this altar in thanksgiving to God, for Noë knew that this was the way to please God the most. (Genesis 8 : 15–20)

Write in your Project Book the story of how God saved Noë.

Sometimes rich people build altars or churches to thank God for His goodness to them.

Of course, while you are a child, you cannot build churches or church altars to honor God. But if you would like to build an altar to show honor to God, you can do this by building a little one in your own room.

Now read several other stories, which will show how mighty God is.

GOD'S POWER RAISES UP A LEADER

At one time when God's people were living in the land of Egypt, the Egyptian king treated them very, very cruelly. They were like slaves.
The people begged God to save them.
And God promised that He would do it.

It was God's plan, in those days, to give the Light of Grace without Baptism to those of His people who believed in Him and were faithful to His law.
For Baptism had not been instituted.
God made Moses the leader of His people.
And He gave Moses the Light of Grace so that he could share in God's Own Light and Beauty.

When God made Moses the leader of His people, " Moses said to God: Lo, I shall go . . . and say to them : The God of your fathers hath sent me to you.

If they should say to me: What is his name? what shall I say to them?

God said to Moses: I AM WHO AM."

And God said: " Thus shalt thou say . . . He WHO IS, hath sent me to you."   (Exodus 3 : 1 3, 1 4)

Then from time to time God sent Moses to the Egyptian king with messages, begging him not to be so cruel to His people, and to allow them to worship Him in their own way.

But the Egyptian king was hard-hearted and would not heed God's messages.

GOD STRIKES EGYPT WITH WONDERS

Then God said to Moses:

" I know that the king of Egypt will not let you go, but by a mighty hand."

So "I . . . will strike Egypt with all my wonders
. . . : after these he will let you go."   (Exodus 3 :
19, 20)
After a while God began to "strike Egypt with
. . . wonders."

The First Plague

And this is what happened in Egypt.
All the waters of the rivers were changed into blood.
And when the Egyptians drank the water, they be-
came sick.   (Exodus 7 : 15–25)

The word "Exodus" tells you that these stories
about the plagues are found in a book of The Bible
called Exodus.

Of course, after this the Egyptian king said that he
was sorry, and he promised to do all that Moses
asked.
But he did not keep his word.
Then God began again to "strike Egypt with . . .
wonders."

The Plague of Frogs

This time a plague of frogs came upon the land.
Frogs were everywhere.
They filled all the land, the rivers, and the houses.

They were even in the places where the people slept. There must have been millions and millions of frogs! And the people could do nothing to make them go away.

Then " Pharao called Moses . . . and said : Pray ye to the Lord to take away the frogs from me and from my people; and I will let the people go to sacrifice to the Lord.

And Moses cried to the Lord . . . And the Lord did according to the word of Moses : and the frogs died out of the houses, and out of the villages, and out of the fields." (Exodus 8 : 8, 12, 13)

But after a while the Egyptian king again forgot his promise!

He treated God's people more cruelly than ever.

Then God began again to " strike Egypt with . . . wonders."

Other plagues came upon the Egyptians and their king.

The Plague of Darkness

One of these plagues was the plague of darkness.

The whole land of Egypt was covered with a horrible darkness.

It was so dark that no Egyptian could see anyone or

anything.　Not one of them moved from the place where he was.

But it was not so with God's people.

Where they were, it was light.　They could see, and they moved about just the same as before.　(Exodus 10 : 21–29)

All of these stories teach us that there is Someone Who is more mighty and powerful than anyone living upon this earth.

Who is this Mighty One?

God is the Mighty One.

Write in your Project Book the reason why God showed His might in Egypt.

Ten plagues came upon the land of Egypt.

In this lesson you have learned the story of three of these plagues.

Ask your teacher to let you have as many story hours in your Catechism class as will be needed to tell about the ten plagues.

After these stories have been told in class, write a little about each plague in your Project Book.

God always heard the prayer of Moses.

When Pharao asked Moses to pray to God that a

plague would stop, Moses prayed and the plague always stopped.

Have your mother or your teacher read to you from the book of Exodus the Bible verses telling how God always heard the prayer of Moses. (Exodus 8 : 28–32; 9 : 27–30, 33; and 10 : 16–20)

A Bible Puzzle: Noë and Moses

In column A on page 64 you will find 7 questions.

The answers to these questions are in column B, marked *From The Bible.*

Read sentence 1 in column A.

Then look down column B. The first four answers do not belong with sentence 1.

But the sentence numbered 12 is right. The question and answer match in this way: God told Noë: "I will destroy man whom I have created, from the face of the earth."

Now find the answer to each of the other questions in column A.

COLUMN A	COLUMN B
Questions	*From The Bible*
1. God told Noë what He would do to wicked people. (What?)	8. God.
2. A book of The Bible tells about the deluge. (Which?)	9. "Let my people go to sacrifice to me."
3. When the plague of frogs was upon the land of Egypt, Pharao asked Moses to pray to God to take away the frogs. Moses prayed, and something happened. (What?)	10. "Make thee an ark of timber planks."
4. A book of The Bible tells about the plagues. (Which?)	11. The book of Genesis.
5. God told Moses what He wanted His people to do. (What?)	12. "I will destroy man whom I have created, from the face of the earth."
6. Someone said to Moses: "I have seen the affliction of my people in Egypt, and I have heard their cry." (Who?)	13. "And the Lord did according to the word of Moses: and the frogs died out of the houses, and out of the fields."
7. God told Noë to make an ark. (Of what?)	14. The book of Exodus.

If you have 5 sentences correctly matched, that is FAIR.

If you have 6 sentences correctly matched, that is GOOD.

If you have 7 sentences correctly matched, that is PERFECT.

THE WATERS OF THE SEA OBEY

Let me tell you another story about God's people and the cruel Egyptians.

It happened while Moses was leading God's people out of the land of Egypt, so that they could worship God as God wanted them to worship Him.

The Egyptians did not want God's people to escape. So they followed them.

God's people were camped on the shores of the Red Sea, when suddenly they saw the Egyptian king and his army following them.

God's people were very much afraid.

They prayed to God to help them.

And God heard their prayer.

He told Moses to lead them forward.

This meant that God's people had to cross the Red Sea. But they had no boats.   And the sea was so big and deep that they could not swim across it.

They did not know what to do.

Just then something happened!

The waters of the Red Sea divided and rolled back.
Then there was a dry path through the middle of the
sea.

And God's people marched on dry land across the
Red Sea!

But as soon as the Egyptians started to follow them
on the dry path, the waters rolled back into place.

The whole Egyptian army was drowned!

But God's people reached the other side in safety.
(Exodus 14:9–31)

Ask your teacher to read this story to you just as it is
written in the book of Exodus.

Write a paragraph in your Project Book, telling how God
saved His people from the Egyptians.

Then write the answer to this question:

Who is the only One mighty enough to have saved God's
people in this way?

THE MIGHTY PROTECTOR

You have been learning about mighty things which
only God can do.

And you have been learning how God always heard
the prayer of Moses and used His mighty power to
protect His people.

Can you think of anything that God is not mighty and powerful enough to do?

There is one word that means that God is *mighty* and *powerful* enough to do *all* things, and that nothing is hard or impossible to Him.

This word is **Almighty.**

Write in your Project Book the new word you have learned. Write what it means.

Copy in your Project Book the statement at the top of page 68, filling in the blank spaces.

—— can do —— things, and —— is hard or impossible to Him.

Look in your Catechism for the question: "Can God do all things?"

Compare your finished statement with the Catechism answer.

You know from this lesson that God wanted Moses to be the leader of His people.
But when Moses was a little baby, the Egyptian king gave a cruel order to kill many babies.
Ask your mother or your teacher to read you the story which tells how God's power protected Moses. (Exodus 2 : 3–11)

Moses wrote a powerful hymn of praise to God the Mighty One. We call this hymn the Canticle of Moses.
Here are some verses from this Canticle.

> " The Lord is my strength and my praise :
> . . . he is my God and I will glorify him :
> the God of my father, and I will exalt him.
> The Lord is as a man of war, Almighty is
> his name." (Exodus 15 : 2, 3)

Write these Bible verses in your Project Book and learn them.

TRUE AND FALSE TEST: GOD IS ALMIGHTY

Divide a page of your Project Book into two equal columns. Write *True* over one column, and *False* over the other.

Read the sentences below, and put the number of each sentence in the column where it belongs.

1. God was not powerful enough to save His people from the Egyptians.
2. God showed His power in the land of Egypt.
3. After God said, "I will strike Egypt with . . . wonders," only three plagues came upon the land of Egypt.
4. God did not save His own people from the cruel Egyptians.
5. God is not Almighty.
6. Nothing is hard or impossible to God.
7. Moses was the leader of God's people.
8. God wanted Moses to be the leader of His people, and God let him share in His Own Light and Beauty.
9. The Egyptians walked across the Red Sea on dry land.
10. Noë was very pleasing to God.

Are your sentences in the right columns?
Ask someone who knows.

Count 10 for each sentence placed correctly.
Mark your score.

Matching Game: Because God Is Almighty

In column A you will find the beginnings of sentences. They are to be completed from column B.

Read number 1. Then find in column B the part that you can add to make a true sentence.

Then do the rest of this matching game.

Write the sentences in your Project Book.

COLUMN A	COLUMN B
1. Because God is Almighty, He gave me a mind —	6. and because God gave me a will, I will always choose Him.
2. Because God is Almighty, He created the earth and everything on it, and —	7. and I am glad that God is my Loving Father.
3. Because God is Almighty, He gave me a will —	8. and because God lets me share in His Own Light and Beauty, I will always act as a noble prince or princess of His kingdom should act.
4. Because God is Almighty, He lets me share in His Own Light and Beauty —	9. and because I have a mind, I will always believe in Him.
5. Because God is Almighty, He made me His child at Baptism —	10. whenever I look at the earth and the things on it, I am glad that God is Almighty.

Each sentence correctly matched counts 20.
What is your score?

GOD·THE·FATHER·ALMIGHTY

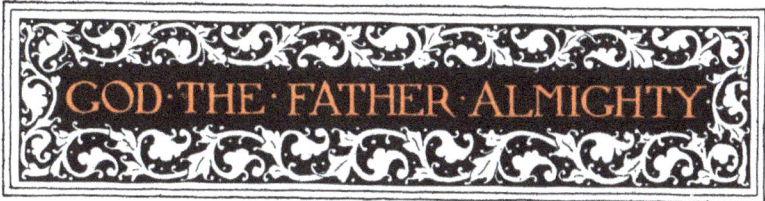

I BELIEVE IN GOD THE FATHER
ALMIGHTY

Before beginning this Topic, you knew that God is our Creator, our Loving Father, our Protector, and the King of Kings.

And in this Topic you have learned something else about God.   What have you learned?

I have learned that God is Almighty.

There is a prayer which begins by telling God that we *believe* He is our *Creator*, our *Father*, and that He is *Almighty*.

This prayer is called the *Apostles' Creed.*

Do you know the Apostles' Creed?

Say the beginning of this prayer.

I believe in God, the Father Almighty, Creator of heaven and earth.

Now let us think for a while about the most perfect of all prayers.

Which prayer is the most perfect of all prayers?

The Lord's Prayer is the most perfect of
all prayers.

No doubt your mother has taught you The Lord's
Prayer, and you already know it.

Whenever you pray, you are talking to Someone.
And when you talk to someone, you should use your
mind to think about the one to whom you are talking.

In The Lord's Prayer, when you are talking to Our
Heavenly Father, what do you say?

I say : " Our Father Who art in heaven."

TRUE AND FALSE TEST: PROBLEMS OF POLITENESS

Arrange this True and False Test in your Project Book
just as you did the one on page 69.

Read each sentence and decide whether it is a true or false
statement. Then put the number of the sentence in the
right column.

1. When I pray, I am talking to my Heavenly Father.
2. When I talk to my Heavenly Father, I should be
   thinking about my school work.
3. When I pray, I should be looking at all the things
   about me.
4. When I talk to my Heavenly Father, I can think about
   anything if my lips say the words.
5. When I say The Lord's Prayer, I think about God.

6. When I talk to my Heavenly Father, I should listen to the radio.
7. When I talk to my Heavenly Father, all my attention should be given to Him.

Ask someone to tell you if your sentences are in the right columns.

> 5 sentences correctly placed: FAIR
> 6 sentences correctly placed: GOOD
> 7 sentences correctly placed: PERFECT
>
> *Mark your score.*

THE PROBLEM OF PRAISE

You have learned about the great King of all the earth.   Who is He?

Our Heavenly Father is the great King of all the earth.

We who are the children of the King should love Him so much that we want His Name to be praised everywhere on the whole earth.
And every day we should pray that everyone in the world will praise Our Heavenly Father's Name.

In The Lord's Prayer, when you ask that Our Heavenly Father's Name may be praised by everyone in the world, what do you say?

I say : " Hallowed be Thy Name."

How I Can Praise God

Fill in the blanks below and make complete sentences by beginning each one with *I can praise God by*.

Copy the completed sentences in your Project Book.

H elping others to praise ——
A ctions brave and —— and ——
L earning as much as I can about ——
L oving ——
O wning books about ——
W riting in my Project Book about ——
E very word I say about ——
D oing what God wants —— —— ——
B eing true to ——
E very "Hallowed —— —— ——" said lovingly
T eaching others about ——
H aving the gift of sharing —— —— —— and ——
Y early giving pennies to the ——
N ever omitting my ——
A sking —— to help me
M any thoughts of ——
E arnestly trying to please ——

Psalms of Praise

In Topic One you learned that in The Bible there are one hundred and fifty beautiful poems called Psalms. Here are some verses from three of these Psalms. Copy them in your Project Book.

Learn them, and you will know the very words King David used to praise God.

" Bless the Lord, O my soul: and let all that is within me bless his holy name.

Bless the Lord, O my soul, and never forget all he hath done for thee."   (Psalm 102 : 1, 2)

" Sing joyfully to God, all the earth: serve ye the Lord with gladness . . .

Praise ye his name : for the Lord is sweet, his mercy endureth for ever. . . ."   (Psalm 99 : 1, 4, 5)

" Praise the Lord, ye children : praise ye the name of the Lord.

Blessed be the name of the Lord, from henceforth now and for ever.

From the rising of the sun unto the going down of the same the name of the Lord is worthy of praise."

(Psalm 112 : 1–3)

THE PROBLEM OF SPREADING
THE KINGDOM

You know that you are the princes and princesses of Our Heavenly Father's kingdom.

And if you are loving princes and princesses, you will want to do all that you can to make Our Heavenly Father's kingdom grow and grow.

So every day you should pray to Our Heavenly Father to give you and everyone else on earth more and more of the very best gift of sharing in His Light and Beauty.

For the more there is of God's Light and Beauty in the souls of people, the more His kingdom will grow.

In The Lord's Prayer, when you pray that Our Heavenly Father's kingdom will grow and grow, what do you say?

I say : " Thy kingdom come."

Matching Game: How to Please the King

Your completed sentences will tell what noble princes and princesses can do to please their King.

Find in column B the part that completes each sentence in column A.

Write the completed sentences in your Project Book.

COLUMN A	COLUMN B
1. They should love their King —	6. of God's Own Light and Beauty in their own souls and in other souls.
2. They should pray for more —	7. to know about the gift of sharing in God's Own Light and Beauty.
3. They should give time, strength, and money —	8. the kingdom of their King grow and grow.
4. They should teach others —	9. to bring God's Light and Beauty into more souls.
5. They should work to make —	10. for giving them a share in His Own Light and Beauty.

Each sentence correctly matched counts 20.
What is your score?

THE PROBLEM OF BEING TRUE TO
THE KING

While you are in God's *earthly* kingdom, there is only one way for you to be happy.

And this way is to do whatever Our Heavenly Father wants you to do.

When you do whatever Our Heavenly Father wants you to do, we say that you are *doing Our Heavenly Father's Will.*

In The Lord's Prayer, when you ask that everyone in the world will do Our Heavenly Father's Will as it is done in heaven, what do you say?

> *I say : " Thy will be done on earth as it is in heaven."*

Now say The Lord's Prayer from the beginning.

THREE PROBLEMS

Write the complete answers to these problems in your Project Book.

1. Every boy and girl knows that he is doing Our Heavenly Father's Will when he obeys his parents.

If he wants to be happy, what will he do when his parents ask him to do something which he does not feel like doing?

The boy in the picture had been playing with the other boys. His mother called him to help the old lady carry

her heavy basket. He did not want to go. But he obeyed his mother cheerfully.

2. Every boy or girl knows that he is doing Our Heavenly Father's Will when he obeys the rules of his school.

If he wants to be happy, what will he do — keep the rules of his school or break them?

3. Every boy or girl knows that he is doing Our Heavenly Father's Will when he obeys the laws of the city or town in which he lives.

If he wants to be happy, what will he do — keep these laws or break them?

Ask your mother or your teacher to read you the story of a young man who obeyed God although he knew that he must disobey the king, who would surely order him to be killed.

This story is in a book of The Bible called Daniel. (Daniel 6 : 3–28)

WHOM SHALL I FEAR ?

A child is never afraid when his father is with him
to protect him, although he may fear many things
when he is alone.

But no child need ever be afraid.
For all through his life, if he keeps the Light of
Grace shining in his soul, he will have with him a
more mighty and powerful Protector than any father
can be to his child.
For the Father of Lights will be the Protector of his
life.

The Bible verse set to Saint Gregory's third tone
asks a question which the melody answers.
You will surely find great joy in singing both the
question and the answer.

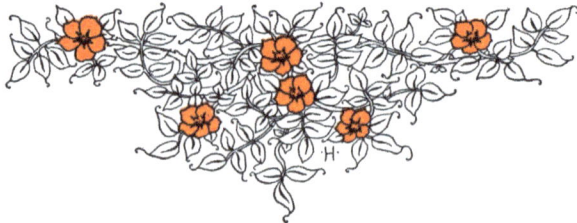

Gregorian Chant: Third Tone   PSALM 26: 1, 2

The Lord is my light and my sal-va-tion, whom shall I fear?

Melody: CORNELIA S. CRANE

The Lord is the pro-tec-tor of my

life: of whom shall I be a-fraid?

THE ONE WHOSE LIGHT CAN SOLVE THE PROBLEMS OF ALL PEOPLE

TOPIC FOUR

BEFORE you begin this lesson, say the Apostles' Creed as far as you have learned it.

Think about the stories you read in Topic Three, which show that God is Almighty.

Who is the only One mighty and powerful enough to have done what these stories tell?

The only One mighty and powerful enough is God.

You have also learned that God showed His almighty power by making heaven and earth, and all things, out of nothing.

Who is the only One Who can make things out of nothing?

God is the only One Who can make things out of nothing.

Now let us learn something more about God.

You know that when God created you, He gave you many wonderful gifts.

Because of one of the gifts God gave you, you have the power *to think.*

ARE MY THOUGHTS SECRET?

Perhaps you did something last summer which made you very happy.

Or perhaps you did something which made you unhappy.

Think about this for a little while.

Can anyone see what you are thinking?

No one can see what I am thinking.

If you want anyone to know what you are thinking, what must you do?

I must tell what I am thinking.

Could Anyone See Marie's Thoughts?

Suppose Marie's mother told her something very important. And she asked Marie not to tell the secret.

Marie let Florence know, but told her that it was a secret.

Soon after this, Marie's mother asked her if she had kept the secret.

Marie knew her mother could not find out that she

had told Florence, because Florence had moved away.

The first thought that came into Marie's mind was to tell her mother that she had not told anyone.

But then this thought came: "A true princess of God's kingdom always tells the truth."

Marie told her mother the truth.

Was Marie's mother able to see what Marie was thinking?

> *Marie's mother could not see what Marie was thinking.*

Unless Marie told, could any of her friends know what she was thinking?

> *Unless Marie told, none of her friends could know what she was thinking.*

See if you can write this story in your Project Book from memory. Be sure to tell what thought came into Marie's mind which made her tell the truth.

You have learned that there is One Who has the power *to do* all things.

Who has the power to do all things?

> *God has the power to do all things.*

God is Light, so He also knows all things.

God always *sees* and *knows* all that you are thinking. And God always sees and knows all that everyone is thinking.

Here is a story which perhaps will help you to find out something more about what God sees and knows.

IS CHOOSING SECRET?

Jack was the son of an army officer, and he loved army life. So his father put up a tent in their back yard, which Jack called his camp.

Jack had just been reading the story of Noë. He was very much interested in the part which told that after the flood Noë built an altar to offer thanksgiving to God.

At once, Jack thought that he too would like to build an altar to give honor and thanksgiving to God.

So he built an altar in his tent. His mother gave him some white cloth to cover it.

Then Jack wanted a crucifix, because he had seen crucifixes on church altars.

He knew that there was a crucifix hanging on the wall in his father's study. So he went to ask his father to let him take it.

His father was much surprised, because up to that time Jack had been asking for drums and guns and other things that soldiers use.

But Jack's father did not know what had happened on Jack's First Communion Day.

On that great day the Light of Grace was increased in his soul.

And at the very moment when the Light of Grace was shining brightest, Jack knew that God wanted him in His service. Right then he made up his mind that when he was older he would be a priest.

Jack's father gave him the crucifix, and Jack turned to go.

But just as Jack was leaving, his father said, " To-morrow I will take you out to buy your new uniform so that you will be ready to go back to the military school in the fall."

Ever since Jack had come home for his summer vacation, he had been wanting to ask his father if he could not go to the preparatory seminary in the fall instead of to the military school.

Jack knew that the time had come to let his father know what he wanted to do. So he told him.

His father answered, " But the military school will prepare you to enter West Point. You have always said that you wanted to be an army officer.   When did you choose the preparatory seminary instead of the military school?"

Then Jack told his father about that one great day when he chose to be a priest instead of a soldier.

Until Jack told his father what he wanted to do, could his father know that Jack chose to be a priest?

Jack's father could not know that Jack chose to be a priest until Jack told him.

But Someone could see and know how Jack was choosing.

Who knew, without anyone's telling Him, why Jack did not choose to go back to the military school?

God knew.

Write a paragraph in your Project Book, telling when Jack chose to be a priest instead of a soldier. Also tell how it happened that Jack asked his father if he could go to the preparatory seminary.

Now you have learned that there is only One Who can see and know what we are thinking and choosing. Who always *sees and knows, without anyone's telling Him,* everything that we are thinking?

God sees and knows, without anyone's telling Him, everything that we are thinking.

Who always sees and knows, without anyone's telling Him, how each one of us is choosing?

God always sees and knows, without anyone's telling Him, how each one of us is choosing.

These two stories will help you to understand something else God sees and knows.

A PROBLEM OF TRUTH AND HONOR

This story is about Teresa.
Teresa lived in the country. She went to the country school.
It was a small school, and there were not enough teachers for every class.
So the principal left Teresa's class without any

teacher some of the time. All the boys and girls in the class promised not to whisper or laugh aloud.

If anyone did whisper or laugh aloud, that child was to write a note to the principal, telling the truth about it. This note was to be handed to the principal when the children passed out at the close of school.

Every day the boys and girls of this class whispered and laughed aloud. But only one did as she had promised.

Teresa chose to keep her promise and write the note, because she had been taught that there is One Who always knows whether we keep our promises or not.

Who knew that all the boys and girls of that class had whispered and laughed aloud, and that only Teresa had kept her promise?

God knew.

Who always knows all that everyone *does?*

God always knows all that everyone does.

Write in your Project Book the reasons why you think it was hard for Teresa to keep her promise.

Write what Teresa had been taught which helped her to keep her promise.

So far you have been learning that God alone sees and knows all that we are thinking, all that we are choosing, and all that we are doing.

GOD SEES OUR ACTIONS

One day after school some children were hurrying along to their Catechism Club.

A Sister was at the door, to greet the children as they arrived.

She noticed that little Joseph held a piece of paper tightly in his hand and looked happier than usual.

"What are you holding so tightly, Joseph?" she asked.

Little Joseph looked up with a smile. He gave the paper to the Sister, and said, "Sister, I just showed this to God."

The Sister took the crumpled paper and asked, "What is this, Joseph?"

"It is my first lesson written with ink. I took the paper right into the church before I came to the club."

There seemed to be no one in the church when Joseph ran up to the altar with his first lesson written with ink.

But Joseph knew that Someone was there Who would be pleased to see him.

Who was pleased to see little Joseph coming with his first lesson written with ink?

God was pleased to see little Joseph.

Write a paragraph in your Project Book, telling why you think that God was pleased with what Joseph did.

A PROBLEM OF UNSELFISHNESS

Now let me tell you a story about a girl called Mary. One day at school Mary noticed a new girl in her class.

At recess time the children were having fun playing a game. But they were thoughtless and selfish, and did not ask the new girl to play.

Mary felt very sorry about this. She saw the problem. As soon as the first game was finished, she went over to the new girl and asked her name.

The girl said that her name was Alice.

Mary knew that the other children did not want Alice to play, because she did not know the game. But Mary's mother had taught her always to be kind. So she did not go back to play with the other girls, even when they called her.

She stayed with Alice until the bell rang. And she made Alice very happy, because she spoke so kindly.

Mary and Alice had not seen anyone near enough to them to hear what they were saying.

But Someone was present Who knew that Mary spoke kind words to Alice.

Who knew that Mary spoke kind words?

God knew that Mary spoke kind words.

Who knows every word that everyone *speaks?*

God knows every word that everyone speaks.

Put yourself in Alice's place. Then write a paragraph in your Project Book, telling whether you would wish to act like Mary or like the other girls. Write the reason for your choice.

Tell someone at home the stories about Marie, Jack, Joseph, Teresa, and Mary. Find out which one those at home like best.

TRUE AND FALSE TEST: THE ONE WHO KNOWS ALL

Copy the following sentences in your Project Book.

If the sentence is true, write the word "True" after it. If it is not true, write "False" after it.

Then show your Project Book to someone at home and ask if you have marked the sentences correctly.

1. God is the only One Who can know how we are choosing, if we do not tell.
2. My friends can see what I am thinking.
3. God did not know that the boys and girls in Teresa's class talked and laughed.
4. God knew that Mary spoke kind words to Alice.
5. God did not know that Teresa was the only one in her class who told the truth.

6. God knew, without being told, why Jack chose to go to the preparatory seminary instead of the military school.

7. God was not pleased with little Joseph's first lesson written with ink.

GOD IS ALL–KNOWING

Can you think of anything anywhere in the world that God does not know?

I cannot think of anything anywhere in the world that God does not know.

Because God knows all about everything everywhere, God is *All-knowing*. And it is because God is All-knowing that Saint James calls Him the Father of Lights.

Say the first part of the Apostles' Creed to yourself, and then tell the three words about God that are mentioned in that part of the Creed.

Creator — Father — Almighty.

Tell the word which means that *God knows all things*.

All-knowing.

Now write in your Project Book these four words that are used in speaking of God.

Copy the following statements in your Project Book, filling in the blank spaces.

1. —— sees us and watches over us.
2. God —— all things, even our most secret ——, words, and ——.

Look in your Catechism for these questions:

> " Does God see us ? "
> " Does God know all things ? "

Compare your finished statements with the Catechism answer.

PROBLEMS A TRUE PRINCE OR PRINCESS MUST SOLVE

When a prince or princess of God's kingdom *does* what is right, Who is sure to know this and to be pleased ?

Our Heavenly Father is sure to know and to be pleased.

Why should we be as careful how we act when we are alone as when we are with others ?

We should be as careful how we act when we are alone as when we are with others, because Our Heavenly Father sees and knows all that we do.

When a prince or princess of God's kingdom *says* what is truthful and kind, Who is sure to know about it and to be pleased ?

Our Heavenly Father is sure to know about it and to be pleased.

When a prince or princess of God's kingdom *chooses* what is right, Who is sure to know it and to be pleased?

Our Heavenly Father is sure to know it and to be pleased.

MORE PROBLEMS

Here are some problems to think out. Write in your Project Book complete answers for each problem.

1. Suppose your class in school is taking a test. The teacher is called out of the room for a few minutes.

The boys and girls near you talk and copy one another's work.

You do not know how to answer one question. And your mother has promised to reward you if your paper is perfect.

The girl sitting next to you has finished, and her test paper is on the desk. If you look, you can easily see what she has written.

Will you look at her paper, or not?

What would anyone do who is a real, true prince or princess of God's kingdom?

2. Suppose your class is taking a test, and the teacher is again called out of the room. Just as before, some of the boys and girls talk and copy, although they had promised not to do this.

Grace will not copy or give her work to others. But those around Grace ask for her work, and keep on asking.

At last she says, "What you are doing is not right."

Just then the teacher comes back. She asks if anyone has talked.

No one but Grace tells the truth about the talking. And she says nothing about the others. So Grace is the only one in the whole class who is punished.

Suppose the same thing happened to you that happened to Grace. Would you tell the truth as Grace did, and take the punishment, or would you be silent as the other boys and girls were?

In that class was there any real, true prince or princess of God's kingdom? Give a reason for your answer.

3. Joseph tries to be kind. He learns easily himself, and he does not like to have his friends fail in class. So he does their work for them outside of class. In class, when the teacher asks his neighbor a question, Joseph sometimes whispers the answer to him.

Is it honest for Joseph to try to be kind in this way?

THE PROBLEM OF OUR DAILY BREAD

You have studied the beginning of The Lord's Prayer. Now let us study more of this prayer.

You are sure that our Loving Father knows *all that you need.*

But He wants you to *ask Him for what you need.*

What do you need to make your body grow, and to keep it well and strong ?

I need food.

And you need food for your soul, to make it brighter and more like God.

You also need food for your soul, to make it strong and true enough to choose what Our Heavenly Father wants you to choose.

But the food you need for your soul is of a different kind from the food you need for your body.

Another lesson will tell you about the food you must have to feed God's Life in your soul.

In The Lord's Prayer, when you ask Our Heavenly Father to give you the food you need each day, what do you say ?

I say : " Give us this day our daily bread."

Let us learn a verse from The Bible, telling us that

Our Heavenly Father knows that we need food, and that He will give it to us.

> " Behold the birds of the air, for they neither sow, nor do they reap, nor gather into barns : and your heavenly Father feedeth them. Are not you of much more value than they ? " (Saint Matthew 6 : 26)

Copy this Bible verse in your Project Book.

WHAT IT MEANS TO TRESPASS

John and James were two boys in the same school. James pushed John on the stairs, so that John fell and sprained his ankle.

Because James pushed John, he caused John much suffering.

We say that James *trespassed* against John.

Trespassed is a new word.

I will tell you another story which will help you to know what *trespass* means.

Every afternoon after school Agnes went to Ann's home to play with her.

One day Agnes's mother telephoned, saying that she wished Agnes to come right home.

Ann answered the telephone.

But Ann wanted to keep on playing. So she did not give Agnes her mother's message.

They played an hour longer.

Then Agnes went home. And she found her mother alone and very sick, waiting for her.

You can guess how sorry Agnes felt when her mother told her about the telephone message.

Ann caused Agnes to suffer. And so we say that Ann trespassed against Agnes.

So you see that if any person harms another by what he says or does, we say that he trespasses against that person.

Write this sentence in your Project Book, filling in the blank spaces. Then the sentence will tell you what it means for one person to *trespass* against another.

When any person harms another by what he says or ——, we say that he —— against that person.

If any person says or does anything which Our Heavenly Father does not want done, that is called *trespassing* against Our Heavenly Father.

Write this sentence in your Project Book, filling in the blank spaces. Then this sentence will tell you what it means for any person to *trespass* against Our Heavenly Father.

If any person —— or does anything which Our Heavenly Father does not want done, that is called —— against Our Heavenly Father.

THE PROBLEM OF OUR FORGIVENESS

If John is kind in what he thinks about James, kind in what he says about him, and kind in what he does to him, we say that John *forgives* James for trespassing against him.

And if Agnes is kind in what she thinks about Ann, kind in what she says about her, and kind in what she does to her, we say that Agnes *forgives* Ann for trespassing against her.

Our Heavenly Father wants us to forgive people who trespass against us.

And Our Heavenly Father will *forgive us our trespasses against Him*, if we *forgive people who trespass against us*.

In The Lord's Prayer, when we ask Our Heavenly Father to forgive us our trespasses, what do we say?

We say : " Forgive us our trespasses as we forgive those who trespass against us."

THE PROBLEM OF FIGHTING TEMPTATION

You remember that, besides people, other beings are also chief creatures of God. What do we call these other beings?

They are called angels.

Most of the angels chose to love God and to be true to Him.

But some of the angels chose to please themselves, and they refused to love God.

The bad angels are called *devils*.

You know that you can please or displease Our Heavenly Father by the way you *choose* to think, or act, or speak.

And the devils want you to choose what you know is displeasing to Our Heavenly Father.

If you do what the devils want you to do, we say that you *yield to temptation*.

But the Light of Grace in your soul will always help you to choose right and not yield to temptation.

Here is the problem of Julia's temptation and how she fought it.

Julia was very bright and was always at the head of her class. For God had given her a great deal of power to think and to know.

She belonged to a large family. Her mother often had to work very late at night to keep their home clean and orderly.

Julia's sister Sarah was two years older than Julia. God had given Sarah a great deal of the Light of His Grace. And Sarah helped her mother every night before she did her school work.

But Julia never wanted to do any work at all, except her own school work.

So sometimes Sarah's marks at school were not so high as Julia's.

After a while Julia began to forget that it was because God had given her so much power to think and to know that she was brighter than the other girls.

Then the devil began to tempt Julia to think that she was better than Sarah! She was even tempted to feel ashamed of Sarah.

But one day after Holy Communion, when God gave

Julia more of the Light of His Grace, she began to see that the devil was tempting her to be proud, like himself.

And Julia was very much frightened, for she did not want to be proud, like the devil.

Then she asked God to help her. For she knew that with the Light of His Grace she could solve this problem and never yield to the devil's temptation.

Write a paragraph in your Project Book, telling what it means to fight temptation or to yield to it.

Also tell what kind of Light will help you most when fighting temptation.

In The Lord's Prayer, when you ask Our Heavenly Father to help you so that you will not do what the devils want you to do, what do you say?

I say : " Lead us not into temptation."

Say The Lord's Prayer from the beginning.

THE ONE WHO CAN DELIVER US FROM EVIL

In the last part of The Lord's Prayer we ask Our Heavenly Father to protect us and keep us safe from fires, floods, disease, bad people, and evil of every kind, especially an unprepared death.

How do you know that Our Heavenly Father can do this?

Our Heavenly Father can do this because He is Almighty.

We want to be protected from every evil of soul and body. But when we are praying to be delivered from evil, we must always remember that the greatest evil for us is not to have the Light of Grace shining in our souls.

In the last part of The Lord's Prayer, when we ask Our Heavenly Father to keep us safe from fires, floods, disease, bad people, an unprepared death, and evil of every kind, what do we say?

We say : " Deliver us from evil."

We end The Lord's Prayer by saying AMEN.
And the Catechism of the Council of Trent tells us that *Amen* means *Know that thy prayers are heard.*

THE PROBLEM OF PRAYER

In The Lord's Prayer you have learned a way of talking to God which is always good and always pleasing to Him.

But it is also pleasing to God if you sometimes talk to Him using your own words.

Read these verses from The Bible.

" Ask, and it shall be given you : seek, and you shall find : knock, and it shall be opened to you.

For every one that asketh, receiveth ; and he that seeketh, findeth : and to him that knocketh, it shall be opened.

If you then being evil, know how to give good gifts to your children : how much more will your Father who is in heaven, give good things to them that ask him ? " (Saint Matthew 7 : 7, 8, 11)

Copy these verses in your Project Book. They are long to learn. But try to learn them and have someone at home test you.

Ask your mother or your teacher to read to you the story of how God helped Daniel to solve his problem when he was thrown into the lion's den the second time. (Daniel 14 : 22–42)

Here is a story from The Bible showing how God hears the prayers of those who love and trust Him.

God's chosen people spent many years in a desert after they had gone out of the land of Egypt.

During this time they were surprised by Amalec and his men coming to fight against them.

Moses picked some of his best men to fight against Amalec.

And Moses knew that the men he sent would win the battle as long as someone was praying. So he and two other men went to stand on the top of a hill in prayer.

And as long as Moses lifted up his hands in prayer, the chosen ones were able to overcome Amalec. But if he let his hands down a little, Amalec began to win.

After a while Moses became very tired standing with his arms uplifted in prayer. So he sat upon a stone and the two who were with him held up his arms. He prayed in this way until sunset. Then Amalec and his men were put to flight.

The problem of prayer is always solved by loving and trusting God.

Write in your Project Book, in your own words, the stories about Daniel and Moses.

PROBLEMS ANSWERED BY THE LORD'S PRAYER

Write the following statements in your Project Book. After each statement, write that part of The Lord's Prayer which asks Our Heavenly Father for what you want.

1. I want Our Heavenly Father to be obeyed by every person in the world. So I say ——
2. I want Our Heavenly Father's Name to be praised everywhere in the world. So I say ——
3. I do not want to do what the devils want me to do. So I ask Our Heavenly Father to help me, when I say ——
4. I want Our Heavenly Father to forgive me my trespasses against Him. So I say ——
5. I want Our Heavenly Father to protect me and keep me safe from every evil of soul and body. So I say to Our Heavenly Father ——
6. I want my body and my soul to be well and strong, so I say to Our Heavenly Father ——
7. I love Our Heavenly Father, and I want His kingdom to grow and grow. So when I pray, I say ——

Pater noster

OUR FATHER, WHO ART IN HEAVEN, Hallowed be Thy Name. Thy kingdom come. Thy will be done on earth as it is in Heaven. Give us this day our daily bread. And forgive us our trespasses as we forgive those who trespass against us. And lead us not into temptation, But deliver us from evil. Amen.

WHY YOU SHOULD NOT BE AFRAID

All people love birds like the yellow warblers because they are so beautiful, and birds like the thrushes because they sing so sweetly.

But there are some birds, like the sparrows, that are not beautiful and do not sing sweetly. Some people do not want sparrows either in bird houses or in their gardens.

But even sparrows have one true Friend. And this Friend watches over them constantly and protects them always. For The Bible tells us that no sparrow falls to the ground unless this Friend lets it fall.
The Sparrow's Friend is God.
And so the sparrows are not afraid, **even though** nearly all people are against them.

God is more to you than a Friend. He is your Loving Father. And you are a prince or princess of His kingdom. So if you do right you should never be afraid, even though many people are against you.

Sing these beautiful Bible verses, which tell how God watches over and protects the sparrows and you.

Gregorian Chant: Fourth Tone Sт. Matthew 10: 29–31

1. Are not two sparrows sold for a farth-ing?
2. But the very hairs of your head are all num-bered.

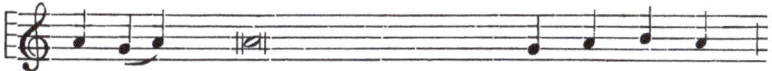

1. And not one of them shall fall on the ground without your Fa-ther.
2. Fear not there-fore:

Melody: Cornelia S. Crane

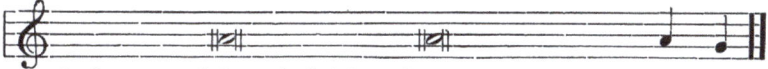

Bet - ter are you than man - y spar - rows.

And now the little ·H· just means that~

these pictures were drawn by
Mother Hackett
Religious of the
Cenacle

www.ingramcontent.com/pod-product-compliance
Lightning Source LLC
Chambersburg PA
CBHW050824090426
42738CB00021B/3475